Your resume is the first writing sample an employer ever sees. In this instance you must consider yourself in sales. The marketing brochure you use to sell yourself is your resume. Making it professional, concise, clear and a true picture of yourself is the goal. It should provide an avenue through which your prospective employer can truly evaluate what you're made of, regardless of whether it's being read by human eyes or one of those fancy software- driven parsing technologies.

The author of this book has professionally written well over 700 resumes. He has 30 years of experience as a hiring manager in multiple fields. During that time he has reviewed multitudes of resumes and cover letters, as well as, conducted several thousand interviews. He has ample practical knowledge of what hiring managers and organizations look for while reviewing resumes.

Listed here is his very comprehensive list of tips on building an eye-catching resume. This list will give you the skills needed to make your resume a winner.

Resume Writing Tips

Determine who will be reading your resume.

If you know who is going to read the resume you are going to submit, then you would be able to decide on the kind of content you want to establish on it. For example, if the resume would go through a Human Resource person, then you simply have to indicate the necessary information, which would make you qualify for the job. However, if it is going directly to the manager or employer, then you will have to be more specific.

Make your resume easy for a person to read.

You have to keep in mind that in most cases your resume is just one of the many resumes submitted on a daily basis to the company you want to work for. Thus, the person reading it may simply get a quick glimpse of your resume to make a decision. If it is not easy to read, then it may get tossed out by the person easily.

Include the details that the reader wants to hear from you.

It is very important that you become more familiar with the requirements of the company when it comes to hiring you. This is because it can help you determine the more important details that you can include in your resume. For example, if you are applying for a managerial position, then you should focus on indicating related experiences which can help you do the job well.

Make your resume short and direct to the point.

Since there is a huge possibility that you are not the only applicant for the position you want, then you should make your resume short and direct to the point. When a manager reads your resume it is safe to assume that he does not have all day to do that. Thus, he may not have a lot of patience in looking for the information he wants from your resume.

Creating Your Own Winning Resume!

Tips From a Professional Resume Writer

Determine the very purpose of the resume.

Although you are making the resume to get the job you want, it is actually just the first step that you are going to take in the process. Thus, the very purpose of the resume is to get your potential employer to contact you for an interview. Once that happens, you can then focus on your interview performance to land on the job you have been dreaming of.

Provide examples to back up your strengths and qualities.

Many people create resumes and list their strengths and qualities like being creative, a problem solver, a hard worker and such. However, this actually does not prove anything. Anyone can create a long list like this. What you can do to stand out is to connect them with real experiences you have in your work or life in general. This illustrates that you do have such qualities.

Determine your priorities.

In coming up with your resume, you have to determine what you really want so as to make something that is really effective. You need to determine whether you want a job for career advancement or to simply earn money. By doing that, you would eventually see the steps that you need to take in order to reach your goals.

Take some time.

Take your time in coming up with your resume for the job you want to apply for. Make up a rough draft of it, perhaps in the form of a word document, before finalizing it. While checking your draft, you should check out not just its content, but also how you have formatted it. Formatting is also important when it comes to considering the reader's experience in checking it out.

Do your research.

If it is going to be your first time to create your resume, you should do your research about it. There are lots of books as well as websites, which can provide you with resume samples. By checking them out, you would be able to have something which you can base your resume on.

Double-check the information.

Before finalizing your resume, you should thoroughly check its content so that you can ensure that it is free from errors. You need to see to it that the dates, the numbers and all the other data it contains is correct. When a resume is free from errors, you are increasing your chances of getting the job that you want.

Make up your mind about the job.

Prior to submitting your resume, you should properly assess if you really want the job that you are applying for. Although you may qualify for it and you are confident that you are going to get it, it is still best if you land on a job that you really wanted in the first place. This would ensure that you would have the necessary drive to excel on the job and be involved with it for a long time.

Applying for many jobs.

Lots of people today send out resumes to almost every hiring company that they come across. They do it with the notion that the more resumes they submit, the more chances they have in landing a job. Although it is true, it may also increase your chances of landing a job which you really do not like. Think very hard before employing this strategy.

What to do in responding to job postings.

Whether you have found the job postings through the internet or locally, it is very important that you read thoroughly to obtain the necessary details. Check out where the company is located, the date that they would start to receive resumes and such. If you feel that there are some details that you need that are not indicated, make use of their contact information and call them.

Learn more about the position.

Before coming up with your resume, you should learn more about the position that you are applying for. When you do that, you would be able to determine whether you are really qualified for it or not. Aside from that, you should also try to check if you do have past experiences which can help you in the job should you get hired for it.

Know your potential employer.

Do your research about the company you want to work for. When you gather information about your potential employer don't forget to check out its mission and vision statements and understand them properly. Aside from that, you should also try to learn more about the kind of working environment the company is trying to develop.

If you want a long term job.

If you are applying for a job position that you want to get involved with for a long period of time, you should carefully select your potential employer prior to coming up with your resume. Choose an employer that has been in business for quite some time. That way you are assured about its stability. Aside from that, don't forget to indicate in your resume qualities of an employee that is committed enough for long term involvement.

Coming up with your main resume heading.

There are lots of options that you have when it comes to your main resume headings. You can choose to have headings that show your qualifications, work experiences, skills, languages and such. Some people also start with their objective; however, this one may be omitted since it is quite obvious that the objective of your resume is to get the job or to get interviewed.

Seek help from a friend.

If you are having a hard time in trying to come up with a resume format that you can start with, don't forget that you can always ask your friends about it. Approach a friend who has successfully landed on the job he wanted and check out his resume. Just take note of the format and start from there.

Adding more headings.

When you have other specific headings that you want to add on your resume, you should consider whether your potential employer is interested in it or not. For example, if the company you are going to apply for a job for is involved with computers, then adding a "Computer Skills" heading could be a good idea.

Make use of quality paper.

One of the first things that employers would notice about the resume is the quality of paper that is used. There is no need to go with the more expensive ones. It is best to focus on quality, and veer away from papers, which may have certain scents. Focus on papers that are quite sturdy, so that the reader won't have difficulties in reading it.

Uncover unstated needs.

In job postings, you can be assured that the company that made it has unstated needs and they may base hiring their employees on that. Therefore, you should try to do more research about the position so you can uncover their unstated needs. If you are able to do that, then you can improve your chances in getting the job you want.

Submit your resume to an online job portal.

There are lots of potential employers today which depend on certain job portals to find people to hire. Thus, it is best if you submit your resume to these job portals. This way, aside from hunting for the job that you want, you can also let potential employers find you.

Using keywords for your resume.

In submitting your resume to online job websites, it is best if you make use of certain keywords to increase the chances of companies in finding it. Many companies already make use of online databases to find potential employees. By making your resume easier to find with the right keywords, you are also improving your potential in getting the job you want.

Using the right titles.

Since people who are tasked in selecting potential candidates for the jobs they posted also are pressed for time, they only take a few seconds in checking out your resume. Thus, you should focus the titles or headings to grab their interest. Use the right description so that employers can become more familiar about your background by simply looking at them.

Proofreading your resume.

The importance of proofreading your resume cannot be overemphasized. Just a small error on it can end your chances of getting the job. Thus, it is best if you proofread your resume at least twice before submitting it. If you have a resume that is short and precise, proofreading it would not take you too much time.

How to shorten your resume.

Since most employers do not have the time nor the patience to read through long paragraphs, you should make use of bullet points in your resume. Using bullet points and numbering can actually help you in summarizing all the things you want your potential employer to know about you. With them, reading it a more pleasant experience to your potential employer.

Establishing the right resume order.

When it comes to having the right order for your resume, you should come up with the most important information first. For example, if you deem that your work experience is the area that is most important for your employer, you should put it at the top. This should also apply in enumerating skills that you have gained through your experiences or trainings.

Determine your direction.

Indicating certain things in your resume which can help your employer learn more about where you are going could also improve your chances of landing the job. This is because employers want to hire employees who have clear pictures of what direction they want to take in their lives. Thus, indicating your professional goals can be a wise decision. At least make your resume in a way that communicates them.

The Font.

Since there are lots of fonts you can choose from in writing your resume, it is best if you focus on certain guidelines. One of the most important things about writing a resume is to make it as clear as possible so that the reader won't have difficulties in reading it. Thus, when it comes to the size of your font, you should focus on 11 or 12. Arial and Times New Roman are good choices for the style.

Availability for job interview.

In submitting your resume, it is best that you tell your potential employer about your availability for a job interview. Aside from that, you should also indicate that you can always provide references when needed. Since you have indicated these things, you should also be prepared in receiving a call for an interview, as well as for your references.

Listing down your skills.

Simply enumerating your skills may not get the job done. Thus, instead of simply enumerating them, you should also state how the company can benefit from them to catch their attention. Doing that would make your potential employers think about the things you have stated.

Always focus on the positive.

Avoid any kind of information which can promote negativity, whether in your experiences or about yourself, when you write your resume. This is also applicable when it comes to being interviewed. If you are asked about your previous employer, you should not mentioned any kind of negativity about them.

Attaching pictures.

Gone are the days when attaching a picture in a resume is of prime importance. This is because most employers are not interested in how you look, unless you are applying for an acting or modeling position which focuses more on the physical traits of individuals. Most employers these days are more interested in your skills and experiences and how you present the information to them through your resume.

Listing responsibilities.

Although listing responsibilities under your experiences is one of the things that lots of people are doing today, you can actually make it better by listing achievements instead. Most employers are already quite familiar when it comes to the functions of a certain position. Thus, listing the responsibilities may not attract their attention as much as your achievements would.

Tailor your resume for the position.

Many people these days follow a practice where they create a generic form of a resume and send it out to as many potential employers as they can. Although this kind of practice can save you time, it may bring down your chances of landing an interview. The best way is to tailor fit your resume to each company you send it to. That way you increase your potential of getting a call for interview.

Use numbers.

If you are going to list your achievements in your resume, utilize numbers in illustrating them. For example, indicating a certain percentage of how much you helped the company in terms of its revenue generated would illustrate it better than a generic statement. By doing this it indicates that you are stating a fact and not just any old claim.

Be more specific.

When you come up with a resume you should be specific about matching your experience and skills. For example, don't just state that you have gone the extra mile in helping a customer. You should indicate the steps you took in helping that customer.

Identify the problems of your potential employer.

Identifying the problems of the company you want to work for can help you in landing the job you want. Check out the kind of industry the company belongs to. For example, if one of the issues the company is currently facing is about its marketing efforts, you you can highlight skills you have to address this need.

Listing your work experiences.

There is no need to list all your past work experiences, especially if you are not very proud about some of them. Focus more on listing your work experiences which are relevant to the kind of position for which you are applying. Also avoid those experiences which only lasted for a couple of months.

Including your age in your resume.

In most countries around the world age discrimination is actually considered illegal. However, unfortunately many companies still consider age as a factor in hiring their employees. It is wise not to include your age in your resume.

Selling yourself.

Your resume is actually all about selling yourself to your potential employer so that they will be convinced in giving you a shot for an interview. Thus, you should focus on this kind of mindset in writing your resume. However, you should also avoid overdoing it. Overselling oneself can also bring down your chances of getting hired.

Go for it.

Even if you still do not have any kind of real working experience, you should not hesitate in applying for the job you want. As long as you truly believe you are qualified, go for it. Just indicate your volunteer work, summer jobs, or training that are especially relevant to the job you want.

Don't lie on your resume.

Although people are pretty much aware of the consequences of it, many still lie in their resumes and even in their job interviews. You have to keep in mind that employers today, especially those who belong to the HR department, have ways of checking out your background. Thus, if they find out about your lie, chances are you won't be interviewed or hired. Aside from that, lying on your resume can also cost you your reputation for good.

Excluding irrelevant information.

Many companies these days do not pay attention to a potential employee's religion, political affiliation, and such. Thus, such information can be considered as irrelevant since they just consume more space in your resume without helping you. Therefore, it is best to skip these facts so that you won't be wasting your time, as well as, your potential employer's.

Considerations to have.

In writing your resume, you should have a number of things you need to consider while doing it. Aside from considering the kind of job you want, you should also consider the kind of salary you are aiming for, as well as, the job's level of responsibility. Doing that would help you come up with a resume that will provide an image matching the things you are aiming for.

Reading job ads.

When you check out the job advertisement that the company you want to work for has posted it will actually provide you with lots of helpful information. Aside from taking note of the qualifications they want, you can also check out what kind of business they are involved with. By knowing that, you would be able to see what they have in common with other companies and determine the kind of employee they are searching for.

Pages in your resume.

Lots of people debate about the length of their resume. Some say the longer the better... while others say to go with a shorter document. What you should take note of though is that employers usually do not have time for lengthy resumes and application letters. Thus, it is best to make it as short as possible. A single page or two can do and get you the interview you are waiting for.

Reviewing your resume.

It is always best to review your resume more than just once. However, it is better to have someone take a look at it before you submit it to the company. There are times when you will not be able to see your own mistakes. An impartial friend would be able to help you out with this. Just keep in mind that no matter what they suggest it is still you who will make the final decision.

Use your best printer.

If you have a number of printers in your house, you should use the best one for your resume. If you have a laser printer, you should know that it is the best kind of printer for resumes. Print out your resume on plain white paper of good quality and avoid any fancy stuff.

Designing your resume.

You resume's design should be as simple as possible. There are actually lots of sample of resumes you can find on the web these days on which you can base your design. If you want to start on it from scratch though, you should keep in mind that you need to avoid fonts that are too small. Aside from that, you should also be consistent in style throughout.

Coloring your resume text.

When it comes to the color of the text in your resume, you should make use of black for it. This is because using that color combined with a plain white paper would make the resume appear as professional as possible. Aside from that, you need to consider that many employers will photocopy your resume, especially if they are scheduling you for an interview.

Become more selective.

If you have just done a rough draft of your resume and you found out that it is too lengthy, being selective can actually help in cutting its length down. Being selective means that you should only include information on your resume that is relevant to the position for which you are applying. Thus, when you scan through it again and find sentences that do not have any purpose, take them out.

Assumptions.

When you read your resume you may immediately make assumptions that it is clear and very understandable. However, you have to make sure that it is understandable not just for you, but also to the reader. Thus, you should recheck it over and over again, and have someone else take a look at it as well.

Describing your previous work experience.

When it comes to providing the details of your past work experience, you can actually indicate the responsibilities that you had. However, it is also best that the person reading your resume be able to understand what kind of business your previous employer was involved with. To address that, you can actually indicate the web address of your past employer's website so that your potential employer can check it out themselves.

Some of your past jobs may be more relevant than the others.

Some people mistakenly consume lots of space in their resumes for emphasizing jobs which are not relevant to the position they are applying for. Thus, it is best that prior to writing your past work experiences you should jot down those that you want to focus on more.

Gather your thoughts.

Before you even start writing your resume you should gather your thoughts about the information you are going to provide in it. This would help you have the right mindset in coming up with the resume that you really want. Aside from that, it will also help in making your resume writing experience a smoother one.

Updating your resume.

It is always best to keep a digital copy of your resume on hand. With this you will be able to update it anytime you want. Updating will mean adding more relevant content to your resume such as new training experiences, academic programs and such. By doing this you are ensuring that you are not missing out in mentioning important details.

Mentioning people you worked for.

If you have the experience in reporting or working with top executives in the industry you belong to, mentioning their names on your resume would not be a bad idea. Make sure though that it is fine with them in case your potential employer would try contact them for confirmation. Aside from mentioning them, you can also ask them to become your character references.

Come up with a resume that does not provide a negative impression.

When it comes to the types of jobs that you have been involved with, you should only indicate those that are of the same type, if you've had jobs in various areas. Aside from that, you should not indicate those jobs you had before which were short termed. This is because employers want to hire people who are decided on the kind of work they want. They also long for people who want to get involved with them on a long term basis.

Avoid jargon as much as possible.

If you are a technical person, you need to keep in mind that when you submit your resume there is a big possibility that the manager that will view it is non-technical. Thus, it is best to avoid technical jargon in your resume as much as possible. This is because your potential employer may not want to spend extra time on your resume by researching about the words that you have used in it.

Position the text in your resume as clear as possible.

Although it is a good idea to come up with a resume that is only a page length you should also make sure that you don't cram too much text in it. Therefore, you should provide good spaces between the words and the lines in your resume. Doing this may make your single paged resume to two pages, but it will become more presentable and less confusing.

When you had years of experience in a particular company.

If you have been with a particular company for quite some time and have been promoted a number of instances, you should list all your positions in it. List your roles and positions you have attained in the company which may have developed your skills further. Doing this can increase your chances in getting the interview or job, .

Online sample resume templates.

When you search through the internet you may find lots of websites which offer free resume samples that you can use as templates. However, you need to be careful in making use of them. Some might be designed for specific positions which you may not be applying for. Sticking with sample templates like those online may also make your resume look more generic.

Your old work experiences.

If you have been working for 10 to 15 years already then there is a big chance that you have already been promoted to different positions. Thus, it may no longer be necessary to list your past working experiences from when you were still starting out. It is best to focus on the most current job experiences that you have... especially those that are relevant to the position that you want.

Fancy designs.

There is no need to make use of fancy designs when it comes to writing your resume. Cute little flowers may appeal to you, but it will not have the same appeal to your potential employers. It can even make your document less professional.

The most important parts of your resume.

Two of the most important parts of your resume would be your name and your contact details. Thus, your name should be the first thing that appears on it at the top. This should be immediately followed by your contact details. If you have more than two pages in your resume they should still appear on the other pages.

How to showcase your accomplishments properly.

Indicating your accomplishments on your resume may not be enough to impress your prospective employer. To properly present them, you should start with stating an issue or a problem that you were able to solve. Discuss the steps you took which solved the problem and were successful.

Focusing on actions.

When you write your resume, it is best to use action words or verbs. By doing that you will sound more proactive. Although resumes are based on the past, you should also make it in a way that it will sound like it is aimed for the future. This is a way that impresses most prospective employers.

Writing numbers.

If you want to become more specific on your achievements by stating certain numbers to illustrate it, it is best that you write the actual numbers instead of doing it by words. Writing numbers such as "$100,000" instead of using "one hundred thousand dollars" will create a better impact on your readers.

Including education.

You educational attainment is also a very important piece of information that you want to include in your resume. However, stating the kind of degree that you have achieved may not be enough. It is best if you can supplement it with something which can indicate that you have worked while studying, obtained further training or have done other productive activities.

The associations you were involved in.

Some people think that including associations in the resume is not necessary. On the contrary, it is actually one of the important items to include, especially if the kind of company you are applying for encourages their employees to develop their people skills or teamwork.

Necessary documents.

When you indicate certain educational attainments, such as a degree you earned or more, you should be prepared in providing the necessary supporting documents for it. Although most employers may not ask for such documents at the initial stages of the hiring process, it is still better to get them prepared if needed further on in the hiring process.

Summarizing your qualifications.

Providing a section in your resume to summarize your qualifications can offer you the edge that you need over your competition. This is very possible especially if you are able to do it properly. When you write down your summary of qualifications you should keep in mind that some employers may just choose to read it, instead of the entire document. A simple list may do.

Saving a copy of your resume.

Saving your resume on your desktop is a good idea since it would make it very convenient for you to update it. However, it is also better if you have a back up plan incase your computer gets infected with a virus or something else. What you can actually do is to save your resume online. This can be done by simply attaching it to your email and sending it to yourself.

Rearranging your resume.

If you are not satisfied with the outcome of your resume, there are lots of things that you can do to remedy the situation. One of which would be to rearrange your resume. This may not change the content of your resume, but it can improve its overall effect, as well as its appearance.

Emphasizing your strengths.

When you want to emphasize your strengths such as indicating that you have "strong leadership skills" or "excellent attention to details", you need to be cautious. This is because anybody can actually do that. However, to make sure that you make a good impression, you should ensure that the rest of your resume will support what you indicated.

Using the objective section.

For lots of people the objective section of the resume can be the most confusing part. You have two choices when it comes to it. You can either omit it or include it in your resume. If you choose to include it, you should consider the objective of the company in writing your own objective.

Show that you are interested.

Some people think that one cannot express how interested they are in the position applying for on the resume. However, you can actually do it by simply taking note of a few things. You simply need to become more specific. Focus more on the needs of your future employer. Show you have done your research and you know what you are doing.

Be confident.

Although this tip is usually provided for interviews... being confident in writing your resume could also help you a lot. This is because when you are confident, you won't hesitate to include the necessary things which can make you stand out from the rest. It will also help you attain the right mindset in writing your resume.

Let your new employer recognize the effort you put into your resume.

When your future employer recognizes the effort you have invested into your resume, your chances of being considered for the position will improve. One of the things you can do is to tailor fit your resume to the position you are applying for. Although this may take some time, it is definitely worth it, especially if you can get the job.

Providing an email address.

Due to the fact that most companies are going digital these days, it is best if you can provide them with a contact email address. Your email address should be created in a professional manner. It should contain at least your first name or your initials so the people reading it can associate it to you.

Highlighting.

Do not highlight certain things excessively. A person reading your resume who sees too many words that are bolded, italicized, or underlined can get irritated by it. Thus, you should minimize the use of them. Use them only to highlight very important information such as your name, address and such.

Indicating your cell phone number.

Some people would advise you not to indicate your phone number in your resume. This is because receiving a call from a potential employer can catch you off guard. However, if you do want to include it, you need to be prepared in answering their calls anytime of the day. This is because they could be calling you for an interview.

Submitting the resume with a cover letter.

If you are going to submit your resume with a cover letter there are certain things that you want to take note of. One of which is to properly match your resume with your cover letter layout. In other words, they should have the same font, text size, margins and headings.

How to review your resume properly.

Proofreading your resume several times can actually help in identifying errors in it. However, if you really want to ensure that it is free from errors, you should do something else once you are done writing your resume. After a few hours check it out again since the break will provide you with a fresher mind to double check it for errors.

Questions to ask after reviewing your resume.

Once you are done reviewing your resume a number of times there are certain questions that you want to ask yourself. You should ask whether your resume was compelling enough, professional looking, clear and easy to read, free from grammatical errors and such.

Submitting your resume.

In these modern times there are different ways of submitting your resume to a company. You can submit it by in person, through email, or even through an online job portal. Before submitting it, especially if you are going to do it through email, make sure that it is saved in the right kind of file so your potential employer can open it.

The elements of a resume that can land you an interview.

A resume that can make an employer contact you for an interview is something that is clean, appealing, and something that can soothe even tired eyes. It should also provide a dynamic summary of your qualifications which target the requirements of the job you are applying for.

Do not use "I" in your resume.

Using I and other pronouns in the resume is not a good idea. This is because resumes are best written in the third person point of view. Doing that will make your resume not just more appealing, but also more professional. It will also make it more believable.

Do not use too many articles.

Using too many articles in a resume is not a good idea, especially if you want to save on space. Articles are words like "a", "an" or "the" which can be considered as fillers. By minimizing the use of such words, you won't just be saving space, but it can also make your potential employer focus more on the important things.

Using professional language.

When you apply for a job your resume should sound as professional as possible. Doing it that way will improve your chances of getting hired for the job. Your resume style should send out a message that you are reliable, presentable and professional.

Practice.

Whether you have found the job that you wanted to apply for or not, it is best if you constantly practice and perfect your resume writing skills. This can improve not just your skills in writing resumes, but it can also help you in other things as well.